D0932475

Fossils

by Grace Hansen

abdopublishing.com

Published by Abdo Kids, a division of ABDO, PO Box 398166, Minneapolis, Minnesota 55439.

Printed in the United States of America, North Mankato, Minnesota.

052015

092015

 THIS BOOK CONTAINS
RECYCLED MATERIALS

Photo Credits: AP Images, iStock, Landov Media, Science Source, Shutterstock

Production Contributors: Teddy Borth, Jennie Forsberg, Grace Hansen

Design Contributors: Laura Rask, Dorothy Toth

Library of Congress Control Number: 2014958426

Cataloging-in-Publication Data

Hansen, Grace.

 Fossils / Grace Hansen.

  p. cm. -- (Geology rocks!)

ISBN 978-1-62970-905-5

Includes index.

1. Fossils--Juvenile literature.   I. Title.

560--dc23

                    2014958426

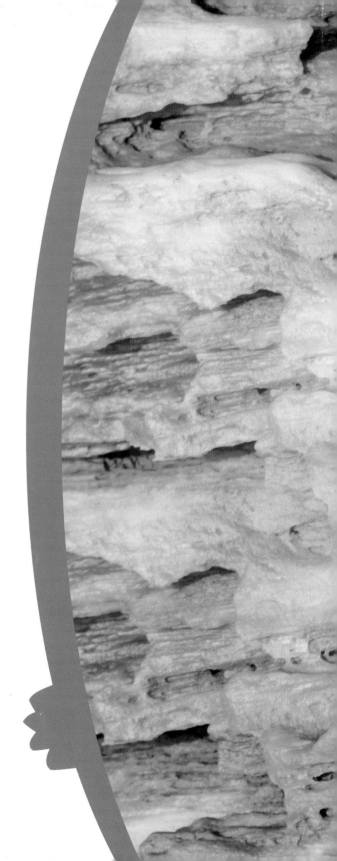

Table of Contents

What is a Fossil?

Fossils can be the **remains** of plants or animals. These are called body fossils. Bones and seeds are body fossils, too.

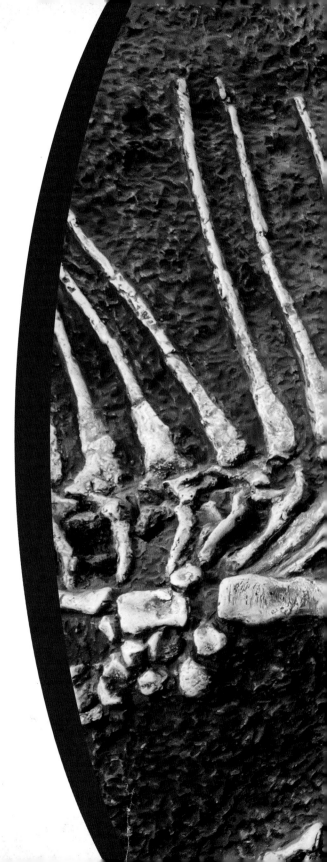

5

Fossils can also show

things that happened.

These are called trace fossils.

Footprints are trace fossils.

6

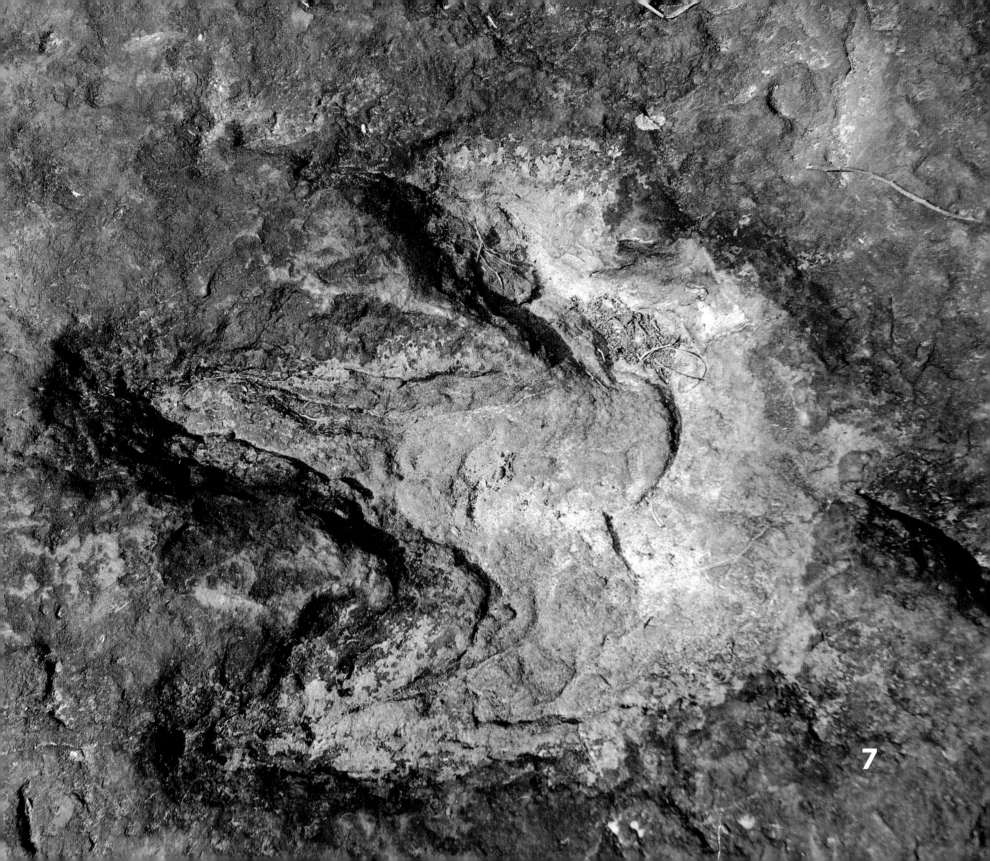
7

Becoming a Fossil

Becoming a fossil is not easy.

Dead animals are often eaten.

Wind can blow dead plants

away. Or they rot away.

9

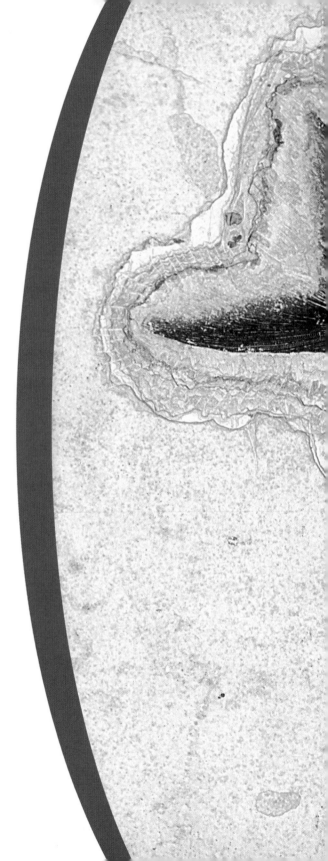

An animal or plant must die in a safe place. Its body must be **protected**.

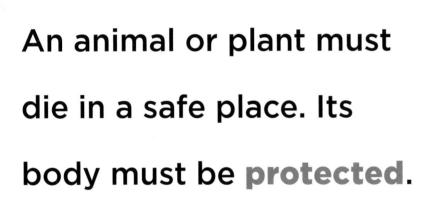

11

To die on a seabed or riverbed is the best. Mud, sand, or soil can easily cover the body. Once covered, the body is **protected**.

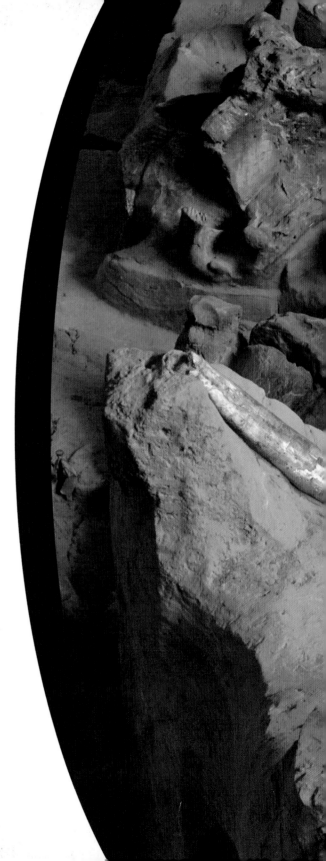

Time passes. The body moves deeper underground. The soil above the body is heavy. It pushes down. The soil around the body turns to rock.

15

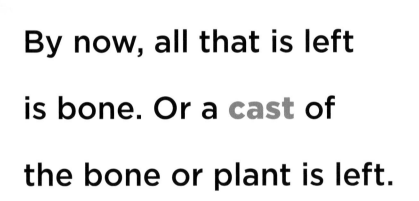

By now, all that is left

is bone. Or a **cast** of

the bone or plant is left.

17

Finding Fossils

Fossils can be found many years later. Special scientists dig up fossils. They must be very careful. Fossils can break easily.

We learn many things from fossils. We learn about how things change. We also learn about Earth's history.

21

Fossil Types

trace fossils

burrow

egg

footprint

body fossils

animal body

plant

shell

22

Glossary

cast – a hollow mold of something.

protect – to keep safe from harm.

remains – what is left of the body after an animal or plant dies.

Index

abdokids.com

Use this code to log on to abdokids.com and access crafts, games, videos, and more!

Abdo Kids Code:
GFK9055